HEALING PRAYERS
for Children in Jesus' Name

Prayers and Photographs Inspired by God,
near Lake Seminole, Donalsonville, Georgia

Gail Thomas and her
Beloved Mama, Jean Castelow

Love and Prayers,
Gail Thomas
and Jean Castelow

ISBN 978-1-64079-755-0 (paperback)
ISBN 978-1-64079-756-7 (digital)

Christian Faith Publishing, Inc.
832 Park Avenue
Meadville, PA 16335
www.christianfaithpublishing.com

Editors
Tiffany Bronson
Sarah Benefield
Carlie Phillips
Tessie Temples
Dr. David Cook

Photographer
Gail Thomas

Special thanks to Christian Faith Publishing Editing Department

Printed in the United States of America

To Jesus Christ

Mrs. Gail and Mrs. Jean believe that the Bible will always be the greatest and most divinely inspired book ever written.

Jesus said, "Let the children come to me, for the Kingdom of Heaven belongs to such as these."
—Matthew 19:14

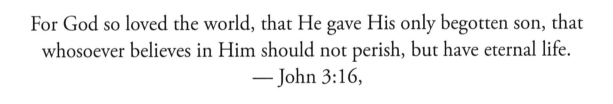

For God so loved the world, that He gave His only begotten son, that whosoever believes in Him should not perish, but have eternal life.
— John 3:16,

Dear God,

I am a little child, but I know that You really love me. Your Holy Bible tells me that I am here for a reason, and You have a special purpose for my life. Help me to call out to Jesus when things are going wrong. I ask for Your wisdom to make good choices as I grow and learn.

Father, give me the peace that I need in my heart today. Give me Your favor in everything that I do. I know that You are working behind the scenes to place Godly people in my path to help me trust in Jesus and be all that I can be for Him.

God, You are so awesome, and I know that I can always run to You when I need to feel better. Thank You for Your great plan for my life and for sending me a loving family.

In Jesus' name,

Your precious child

Dear God,

The Bible says that in the last days, You will pour out Your Spirit upon all people. I am happy to say that I am Your child, and I want to live for You. I know that Jesus healed many people when He was on the earth, and I believe He is still healing people today.

I believe You are a loving Father and that You are pleased with me. I know that You love me, no matter what is going on around me. Father, I give You my whole heart. I will look for Your favor each day. I can expect good things from You, God.

I can trust that You will take care of my family. You are always with me, and I never have to be alone. Jesus is my Shepherd, and I am His little lamb. I will be ready to follow Him, wherever He leads me. He is my Master, and I will always be His precious child.

In Jesus' name,

Your precious child

Dear God,

Help me to want to serve You. Please help me be loving and kind. God, I pray You will give me wisdom to understand Your grace and favor, and no matter what things I have, help me to see they all belong to You. God, use me to help someone every day. Please let me serve Jesus, and bless my dear family.

In Jesus' name,

Your precious child

Dear God,

I come to lift up the name of Jesus. I know that I cannot earn my way to Heaven, but through simple faith in Jesus, I can see my loved ones again someday. Father, thank You for loving me.

Lord, help me to hold my head up, without feeling afraid. I can trust that You will order my steps, and I can walk with Jesus each day. I know You can work things out for good for me and my loved ones.

Lord, You made every bird with their lovely colors. I watch the mother cardinal resting and watching over her little ones. I feel Your loving wings surround me as I rest in Your tender love. I will lay my worries down at the beautiful feet of Jesus, my Savior.

I will never forget what Jesus has done for me. He laid down His life for me. Now I will carry my cross and lay down my life for Him.

In Jesus' name,

Your precious child

Dear God,

As I breathe in the fresh air, I pray to feel peace and joy overflowing my heart. Help me to enjoy this day and to treasure my time with You.

Father, I may not see You, but I feel Your Holy presence. You are always waiting for me to run to You when I'm feeling sad or confused. Help me to remember that You are always watching over me.

I see the baby geese surrounding their loving mother while their protective father watches over His family. God, I know You are watching over my family and wanting good things for our lives. You are my loving father in Heaven.

In Jesus' name,

Your precious child

Father,

I am amazed at the great love that Jesus has for little children. He loves children just like me and makes me part of His royal family. As I walk by the lake, I notice the water lilies blooming along the edge of the water. You make the flowers bloom in Your own time.

Lord, I believe You have a great plan for my life, and I will become who You want me to be. I will praise You always. You are so worthy. Show me that You are real! I will worship You.

In Jesus' name,

Your precious child

Dear Lord,

Sometimes I go through struggles, and I need You to wrap me up in Your loving arms. I want to know Jesus in a personal way, so I can become more and more like Him.

Father, I have laughed many times, and at times, I have cried. You know what I am going through each day. I know that You can hear my prayers. The Bible tells me that Jesus is looking for simple, childlike faith, and that is all I have.

I know I am important and valuable to You. You see every sparrow that falls to the ground. You reach down and gently lift each little bird that falls. I feel You're working things out in my favor. I want to please You in all I say and do. You have been so good to me, and I can feel Your loving hand lifting me gently with Your grace and mercy.

In Jesus' name,

Your precious child

Dear God,

The Bible tells me that nothing is impossible for You, so I place my hope and trust in You. I believe that You sent Your son, Jesus, to pay for my sins. Now I can be righteous in Your sight and walk with You on His earth.

I know You sent Your sweet Holy Spirit to teach me all things and to guide me each day. I feel Your loving angels watching over me as I sleep at night. I am so happy, because Jesus is mine!

In Jesus' name,

Your precious child

Dear Father God,

I give You all the praise and honor today for helping me to learn and grow. Help me to remember the sacrifices my family has made for me and to treat them with respect. Help me to treat others the way I want to be treated each day. I pray that You will help me show kindness to others and that I will have someone in my life to give me gentle guidance.

I will give You all the glory for the beautiful things You made. You sent Jesus, and with Him, I can do all things through Christ who strengthens me.

In Jesus' name,

Your precious child

Dear God,

I give You all the praise and honor today for helping me to learn so many things that I needed to know. Father, help me to pray like I should and to trust that You know what is best for me. Help me to be more patient and praise You for all the things You have made.

Lord, help me to be kind and gentle to others. I know I am loved, because I am Your child. Help me to touch the hearts of everyone I love. Let my little eyes shine for You and my joy spread to others.

Father, help me to dance with joy and let my light shine for Jesus. I wish everybody knew how much You love them. God, please use my life in a special way for Jesus. I pray that I will lift up others in my prayers and with my sweet words. Give me a cheerful heart and a beautiful smile to win others over to Jesus.

In Jesus' name,

Your precious child

Dear God,

I may be a little child, but the Bible tells me that Jesus really loves the little children. I come to give You all of my praises. You are so kind and gentle, and You made all the birds in the sky for me to see.

The Bible says that You feed the birds and take care of them. God, please take care of my family this night. Help us not to be afraid and to trust in You.

In Jesus' name,

Your precious child

Dear Father,

I thank You and praise Your name for all the things You have made. Help me to truly love others and remember Your greatest rule; To love God with all of my heart, mind and soul, and to love my neighbor as myself.

I pray that I will think of what others may be going through and that I will show compassion and mercy. Help me to live through the mighty power of Jesus. His grace teaches me to forgive others, because He has forgiven me. I know I'm not perfect, but You love me anyway.

I can hear music from Your throne as the angels sing praises to Jesus, the King. I will dance and sing with joy. I will lift my little hands up to You in praise and worship. Jesus is everything!

In Jesus' name,

Your precious child

Dear God,

I come to honor You and let You know that I will try to live for Jesus. Your Bible is the divinely inspired word, dear Father. I pray that someone will help me to learn about Jesus as I listen to Bible stories.

Lord, I pray that, as I grow, You will lead me to accept Jesus Christ as my personal Savior. He is so awesome and can be my dearest friend. I am so happy to have Jesus in my heart. His sweet Holy Spirit can teach and guide me each day.

Lord, I am ready to be all that You want me to be. I can feel Your loving arms wrapping around my shoulders as You cover me with Your joy, peace and love. I know You're always near to me.

In Jesus' name,

Your precious child

Dear God,

I come to You in praise and worship and to make my requests known to You. Help me to be peaceful with everybody. Father, help me serve You with joy and to be faithful and honest with others.

God, help me come to Your throne with boldness and never be ashamed that I serve Jesus Christ. Lord, I ask for Your Holy Spirit to guide me on the right path every day. Help me only speak sweet words to others and help me turn away from all wrong things.

Please give me wisdom so I can love and show understanding to help others. Let my light shine, and help me to be Your servant.

In Jesus' name,

Your precious child

Dear God,

I need Your help today, more than I ever have. I want to be able to do so many things, Lord. I find it hard to focus on one thing at a time. I pray that You will help me to take one day at a time and not to be so busy that I do not take time to pray about my problems. God, please forgive me for being so selfish sometimes. I pray that You will use me to reach out to another child who needs my love and acceptance today.

Father, help me to say no when I need to and help me to say kind words to a lonely or hurting child who may feel left out. Help me to ask You for direction and not to worry about what my friends think. Help me to want what You have designed for my life. Help me to be a friend to others and care about children who are struggling.

I pray that You will help me forgive others when they hurt me, like You have forgiven me. I ask that the light of Heaven will shine through my heart. Please let my smile shine for Jesus and let me be His hands and feet on this earth. Father, help me to be humble.

In Jesus' name,

Your precious child

Dear God,

I come to praise and worship You. I want to learn all that I can about Jesus and about His love for me. Lord, help me to be kind and gentle like Your precious Son. I need help learning to be patient and understand that I cannot always have my way.

Lord, I ask that You fill my heart with Your joy. I want to shine as a light for Jesus in this world. Let my smile and eyes light up this earth for You. Please use my life to serve You.

Father, help me to show that I belong to You by the sweet words that I speak. Father, give me peace in my heart as I win others over to Jesus. Help me touch the hearts of others for You. You are so great, and I love You.

In Jesus' name,

Your precious child

Dear Father,

I praise You for Your beautiful birds and for everything You have created. Your work is so awesome. Help me to see Your great plan.

Father, I thank You for sending Jesus. He is my best friend. I can depend on Him through the hard times. My hope and my future are in Your mighty hands. I will give You my all!

In Jesus' name,

Your precious child

Dear Lord,

Help me to be a friend to others who may not have a friend. I pray that You will help me see Your great plan for all of Your children as they give their hearts to Jesus.

I pray that I will love and include all children as a part of the body of Christ. Help me to understand that some children have different needs and that You made each of us for a reason. Jesus taught us to love our neighbors as ourselves. Father, help me to treat other children kindly and pray for them.

Thank You, Lord, that I can feel the love that Jesus has placed in my heart for Your children. I am so glad to know Jesus is my Savior.

In Jesus' name,

Your precious child

Dear God,

I am Your child. I believe Your Holy Word. I pray that You will help me understand Your wonderful purpose for my life. I ask that You will stand beside me through the sunshine and rain. I pray that the storms of life will not overwhelm me.

Father, please send Your strength and peace into my home today. We need Your Holy Spirit to comfort our hearts. Help me to remember that I am very special and created in Your beautiful image. You will draw near to me and give me the strength and peace I need.

You have redeemed me through the precious blood of Jesus, and my relationship with Him has provided a home for me in Heaven one day. I will smile in peace, knowing You are so near. Let my faith grow and show Jesus' love and mercy to others. Use me to help someone see Your awesome power. Let Your creation praise Your majestic name.

In Jesus' name,

Your precious child

Dear God,

The Holy Bible says that we are all children of God. Lord, help me to have faith in You, even though I don't see You. I feel Your warmth in the garden as the pretty butterfly dances from flower to flower.

I pray that I will feel Your healing touch, and You will help my loved ones come to know and love Jesus. Please forgive people who will not accept Your wonderful truth. I know that Jesus died on the cross for me and has been raised up to Heaven. God, help those who do not know You to invite the Holy Spirit to live in their hearts, forever.

In Jesus' name,

Your precious child

Lord,

I pray that I will live my life to please You. Please fill my little heart with Your Holy Spirit and help me remember that You are my Heavenly Father who knows what I need before I even ask.

I can run into Your loving arms when I am hurting. I know that You have anointed me to do great things on this earth. Help me to be excited about Jesus and let others see the joy in my smile each day. Help me to be content with what You have given me and do my best to serve Jesus with my gifts and talents. It brings me such joy to know that Jesus loves me.

In Jesus' name,

Your precious child

Dear Father,

I come to You as Your precious child. I know You gave Your son, Jesus Christ, to perform great miracles on this earth. You make the sun go down and create a beautiful sunset every evening at this beautiful lake. I see the colors in the reflection on the water. It takes my breath away.

You are so awesome, God! I love You with all my heart. I believe You still can do miracles, and You can use ordinary people to do great things to honor Jesus. Nothing is impossible with faith.

Lord, I ask for faith to believe that You can heal my loved ones, if it is Your will. You will always know what is best for Your children. You are in control of my life.

In Jesus' name,

Your precious child

Dear Father,

I've been hurting today. I come to kneel down before You and pray for help with my problems. I know that You control Heaven and earth. You are always setting things up in my favor. You send the right people and help me to make the right choices.

I feel Your presence, and I know You're watching me from Your Heavenly throne. I ask You to humble me and help me to have a sweet attitude with my family and friends. Help me to put others ahead of myself. I will trust You to help me each day.

I know that You care deeply for me, because You sent Your own precious Son Jesus, to show unconditional love. Even when we make mistakes, He forgives us and loves us anyway. Father, I will give You all of my praise and glory for all You've done for my family. Help me to show Your love and acceptance to all others. You are so wonderful! Your mercy is so new and fresh every morning. I love You so much!

In Jesus' name,

Your precious child

Dear Father,

I am amazed as I watch the ospreys in a pond near the lake. The mother and daddy make a huge nest by bringing sticks, one by one. After the eggs are laid by the mother, she sits on them and shades them from the hot sun. The daddy brings fish and food to the babies, after the eggs hatch. The babies love to walk around the nest and learn to fly.

Lord, You are my Heavenly Father, and I know I can depend on You for food and shelter. I feel Your loving arms when I am sad and lonely. I know You send angels to comfort me when I'm afraid. You will always be near to me and will never give up on me. You are so wonderful. Thank You for my family. Help us all to have more faith in Jesus to love You more than ever.

In Jesus' name,

Your precious child

Dear Heavenly Father,

I thank You for sending these prayers and photographs for Your book. I pray that each child who receives a copy of this book will be blessed. I also pray that parents and others who read these prayers and see the photographs will give You all the glory.

In Jesus' name,

Your precious child

Afterword

The authors of this book are Gail Thomas and her dearest angel mama, Jean Castelow, and photographer is Gail, who took these pictures around Lake Seminole.

Gail shares, "My dear Mama will always be my dearest angel. She has been my greatest friend and my encourager all of my life. Without her faith in Jesus, this book would not be possible, but with God, all things are possible."

Gail gives credit to God for the photos, taken during her years at Lake Seminole. Gail's mother prayed for a baby when she was younger and was told she couldn't have one due to health problems. She was able to give birth to Gail and dedicated her to God to do something very special to glorify Him.

Gail taught at Seminole County Elementary School in Donalsonville, Georgia, before retiring, and she noticed that the children she taught seemed fascinated to learn about nature through the photos she shared with them. Gail also credits her mama for taking her to visit people who were less fortunate, taking her to church, teaching her how to pray, reading Bible stories, and teaching her about Jesus. Gail's mama also loved nature and taught her about the wonderful things that God made. Gail has two younger sisters, Rhonda and Sherrie. She also has a husband, Wayne; a son, Jason, and his family; and many nephews and nieces to love. Gail's daddy, William Castelow, passed away in 2008, and he will always be dear to her heart and loved by her family.

After Gail retired, her mama's health worsened, and they spent many hours together, praying and praising God. Gail's Mama taught her how to pray and how to be humble before the Lord. This beautiful lady continued to worship, sing and pray, until she became very ill. Gail's precious mama passed away on August 3, 2016. Her heart was the children's book. Gail and her mama dedicate this book to Jesus.

In 2012, Mrs. Jean had a supernatural experience. Gail and her family were told that she was not going to live much longer. Gail called the ambulance, and they spent two weeks in the Donalsonville Hospital. Mrs. Jean said during that time, she was taken to Heaven and stood before Jesus. She saw loved ones and was also very happy. Jesus told her that He was sending her back to help her daughter finish this children's book. We are so thankful that God used a mother and daughter as vessels to complete a good work. We give Him all the credit, honor, and glory for the photographs and the prayers. Gail is so proud that her mama prayed a blessing over her many years ago.

Gail and her mother would like to thank Tiffany Bronson, senior editor, who did a great job of helping their vision come to life in the children's book. Other editors who helped were Sarah Benefield, Carlie Phillips, Tessie Temples and Dr. David Cook. Also, Gail would like to give a special mention to her wonderful husband, Wayne, and to Pastor Jimmy Dean, who was always there for her precious Mama. A special thanks to Tynese Parks for her love and devotion. Also, our special appreciation to Dr. Josh Walker, Dr. Winston Ortiz, and Dr. Gary Smith.

Most of all, we need to thank our Lord Jesus for all He has done to bring this vision alive and give him all the glory for those who are touched by the words and pictures. We know it all came from God! May God Bless each person who will be helped during difficult times with His healing touch.

Gail's mama had six grandchildren and a granddaughter in Heaven and six great-grandchildren. Jesus loves all children, and always remember: He loves You unconditionally. You can do great things for Jesus too!

ABOUT THE AUTHORS

Gail Thomas is a retired teacher who loves Jesus and was blessed to spend five years with her mama, before she went to be with the Lord. She shared a special blessing with her mother when she returned from her visit to Heaven during a terrible illness and came back telling Gail that she was with Jesus, and He wanted her to encourage Gail to complete this children's prayer book. That is exactly what her mother did daily.

Gail received the prayers supernaturally in 2007, and she had spent time taking photographs of nature around Lake Seminole, near Donalsonville, Georgia, where they lived with Gail's husband, Wayne. Gail and her mother asked a friend named Tiffany to help them combine the pictures and prayers.

Gail also has a son, Jason, and his lovely wife, Jessica, as well as a very precious granddaughter to love. She is also blessed to have nieces and nephews, as well as five great-nephews.

It is Gail's prayer that this book will inspire, encourage and heal people's hearts through the prayers, as well as the photographs. Her mama continues to live on in Gail's heart through this Children's book, all arranged by her Heavenly Father to glorify his Son, Jesus, and for the Holy Spirit, who guided her as she photographed nature and wrote these prayers for children in only one weekend in February, 2007.

Gail and her mama, Jean, would like to give all the credit for this book and the photographs to God, Our Heavenly Father through his son, Jesus Christ! It was their dream that each reader would be touched, knowing that he used ordinary people like them to do something to reach out to all people with love and acceptance. You are deeply loved!